Age of dinosaurs. Dinosaurs are at their peak in size, variety and numbers and dominate every continent.

'K-T extinction'. End of the dinosaurs.

Mesozoic era

248 MYA – 65 MYA

Cretaceous period

144 MYA – 65 MYA

Hadrosaurus
Velociraptor
Protoceratops

Centrosaurus
Troodon
Tyrannosaurus
Triceratops
Ankylosaurus
Edmontosaurus

Giganotosaurus
Spinosaurus

Argentinosaurus
Nodosaurus

Deinonychus

Acrocanthosaurus

Iguanadon

Baryonyx

FULL TIMELINE

Oceans and atmosphere form. Earliest life forms in oceans.

Trilobites dominate seas. Still no land life.

Earliest land plants appear.

Insects flourish. First reptiles evolve. Shrubs, ferns and trees dominate land.

Massive volcanic eruptions cause mass extinctions, wiping out 90% of marine life and 70% of land life!

Precambrian time 4.5–3.9 BYA			Palaeozoic era 540 MYA–248 MYA					
Hadean eon	Archean eon	Proterozoic eon	Cambrian period	Ordovician period	Silurian period	Devonian period	Carboniferous period	Permian period

The Earth forms!

Sea plants begin photosynthesis.

First fish evolve.

Fish dominate oceans. Spiders and mites are first land creatures. First amphibians evolve. First forests form.

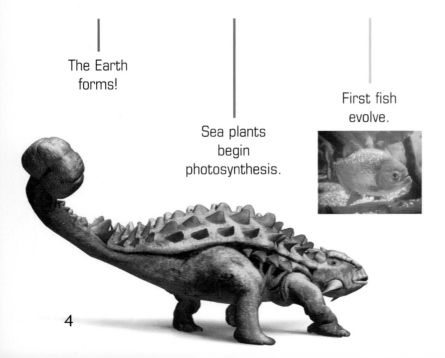

Synapsids, such as Dimetrodon and amphibians such as Eryops dominate land.

Dinosaurs dominate. First mammals evolve.

'K-T extinction' End of the dinosaurs.

Mammals such as horses, bats and whales evolve.

Most modern birds and mammals have evolved.

'Great Ice Age' Neanderthals and Homo sapiens, or modern humans, evolve. Smilodon (sabre-toothed tiger), mastodons and mammoths evolve.

Mesozoic era 248 MYA–65 MYA			Cenozoic era 65 MYA–NOW							
			Tertiary period (65 MYA – 1.8MYA)						Quaternary period (1.8MYA – NOW)	
Triassic period	Jurassic period	Cretaceous period	Paleocene epoch	Eocene epoch	Oligocene epoch	Miocene epoch	Pliocene epoch		Pleistocene epoch	Holocene epoch

Sauropsids such as the archosaurs dominate. First cynodonts such as Cynognathus evolve. Marine reptiles evolve.

Age of dinosaurs. Dinosaurs are at their peak in size, variety and numbers and dominate every continent.

Mammals dominate. Early carnivores evolve.

Creodonts evolve. Modern mammals become dominant.

Hominids, the ape-like ancestors of humans evolve. Thylacosmilus and other early sabre-tooths evolve.

Last ice age ends. Human civilisation develops.

EVOLUTION

The Earth, and all life on it, is constantly changing. Life had been on Earth for at least 3,260 million years before the dinosaurs appeared. The Palaeozoic era was from 540 to 250 million years ago, and was known as 'the age of ancient life'.

By 245–235 million years ago (the Mesozoic era) a large number of reptiles roamed the earth. Some of these were dinosaurs, including herbivorous rhynchosaurs and carnivorous archosaurs.

Dinosaurs appeared about 230 million years ago, during the Triassic period. Their evolution spread over the Jurassic and Cretaceaous periods, a total of 165 million years.

Dinosaurs completely dominated the land in a way that no other group of animals had done. Eight hundred species have been identified so far. No one knows where they came from.

Extinction

About 65 million years ago (the end of the Cretaceous period), 70 per cent of living species, including the dinosaurs and flying reptiles suddenly became extinct. Crocodiles and many other reptiles survived.

Tsunami breaking wave

Dimetrodon

Archaeopteryx

Crocodile

The most popular explanation for this extinction is that an asteroid from space hit earth. There has been evidence of an enormous meteorite colliding with the Earth 65 million years ago. The meteorite may have been a single asteroid, bits from asteroid collisions, or debris from a comet. This would probably have thrown up an enormous amount of dust into the atmosphere which would have blocked out the sun and made the whole world dark for several months.

It might also have caused other natural disasters such as tsunamis and earthquakes. All plant life would have died, therefore plant eaters would not have been able to survive. In turn, carnivores would have had no food, causing them to die.

Other theories include a period of intense volcanic activity which may have caused changes such as global warming and effects on plant life. Another argument is that a drastic drop in sea level would have made the climate more extreme. It is difficult to imagine how this could have had such an effect. A third theory is that the climate changed enough to make earth too cold or hot for reptilian life, but this does not explain how some reptiles, such as crocodiles, survived.

The Cenozoic era began 65 million years ago and is often called the 'age of mammals', because mammals thrived at this time.

Scientists believe that birds are descendants of the dinosaurs. They may have come from small meat eaters such as Compsognathus (see page 62). You can see the similarity, especially when you compare the skeleton of dinosaurs to the skeleton of the oldest known bird, Archaeopteryx, which lived about 140 million years ago.

BRACHIOSAURUS

Tree-top grazing giant

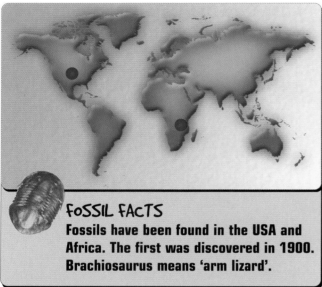

FOSSIL FACTS
Fossils have been found in the USA and Africa. The first was discovered in 1900. Brachiosaurus means 'arm lizard'.

Brachiosaurus was named in 1903 and gets its name from its long front limbs. It was 25 m (82 ft) long and 15 m (49 ft) high.

For many years it was thought to be the world's biggest dinosaur, but recent discoveries – such as Argentinosaurus – were proved to be bigger in terms of sheer mass.

Appearance and diet

Brachiosaurus walked on four legs, had a long neck, tiny head and a comparatively short, thick tail. It had chisel-like teeth to nip leaves and fruit from the trees. It had nostrils on top of its head, which meant it could eat almost constantly without interfering with its breathing. It swallowed its food whole, without chewing.

To help with its digestion, brachiosaurus swallowed stones. These stayed in its gizzard. Tough leaves and plant fibres would be ground up by the stones as they went through.

Circulation system

To pump blood all the way up its long neck to its tiny brain, Brachiosaurus had to have a powerful heart and broad, strong blood vessels, with valves to prevent the blood obeying gravity and flowing backwards. Scientists once thought Brachiosaurus actually had two brains, the second

near the hip area – but current thinking is that this was simply an enlargement in the spinal cord.

Habitat

At first, scientists believed it must have been an aquatic dinosaur, spending all its time in the water and using its long neck and the nostrils on top of its head as a kind of snorkel for breathing. However, studies showed that water pressure would have stopped Brachiosaurus from breathing properly when submerged.

Dinosaur Data

PRONUNCIATION:	BRACK-EE-OH-**SAWR**-US
SUBORDER:	SAUROPODOMORPHA
FAMILY:	BRACHIOSAURIDAE
DESCRIPTION:	LONG-NECKED **HERBIVORE**
FEATURES:	HUGE FRONT LIMBS; TINY HEAD
DIET:	HERBIVORE

MEGA FACTS

- Brachiosaurus may well have lived to be 100 years old.

- It probably travelled in herds.

- Brachiosaurus needed to consume 200 kg (440 lb) of food *every day* to fuel its massive body.

- It weighed 20 times as much as a large elephant!

- A full-size replica of a Brachiosaurus skeleton is mounted in O'Hare International Airport, Chicago.

Scientists now believe that Brachiosaurus lived completely on land. Although their fossilised footprints have been found beside shorelines (they probably went there to drink) they have also been found in areas that 156–145 million years ago would have had very little water.

In 2003, a computer simulation run by Dr Donald Henderson in Canada, showed that Brachiosaurus would have floated rather than sunk if it had fallen into deep water – its hollow backbones would have helped it to float, though it would probably have rolled onto its sides in the water rather than staying upright.

ARGENTINOSAURUS

Gigantic long-necked herbivore

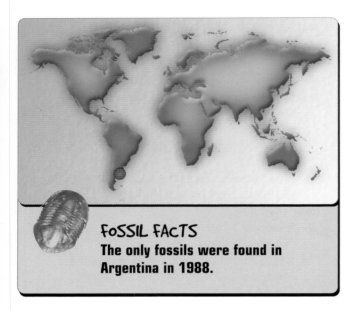

Argentinosaurus means 'lizard from Argentina'. It was named in 1993 by palaeontologists José F. Bonaparte and Rodolfo Coria after the country where it was found.

Appearance

Argentinosaurus may have grown up to 40 m (130 ft) long, 21 m (69 ft) tall and about 9 m (30 ft) wide and weighed 90–110 tons (90,000–110,000 kg).

An entire skeleton has yet to be discovered. Only about 10% of the Argentinosaurus skeleton was found, and nothing at all from its neck or tail. Scientists used the bones that *were* found to work out which other dinosaurs Argentinosaurus was related to. They then made their 'best guesses' at its appearance based on what those other dinosaurs looked like.

It would have looked very similar to a Brachiosaurus with a long tail, and a tiny triangular-shaped head on the end of its long neck. It would have needed a big, powerful heart to pump blood all the way up that long neck to its tiny brain.

Backbone

Scientists think its backbone worked in a special way to support the vast weight of the animal. The backbones interlinked to make the whole back into a sort of bridge of bone.

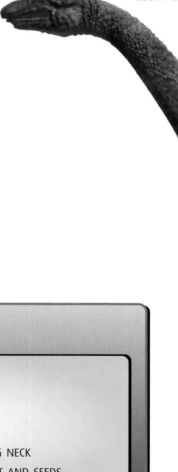

Dinosaur Data

PRONUNCIATION:	AHY-GEN-**TEEN**-OH-**SAWR**-US
SUBORDER:	SAUROPODOMORPHA
FAMILY:	TITANOSAURIA
DESCRIPTION:	GIGANTIC LONG-NECKED HERBIVORE
FEATURES:	SPECIAL INTERLOCKING BACKBONE, LONG NECK
DIET:	MOSTLY CONIFERS, ALSO FLOWERS, FRUIT AND SEEDS

Curiously for such a big animal, the bones were hollow – perhaps they evolved that way to reduce weight and let Argentinosaurus move its vast bulk around more quickly.

Diet

Argentinosaurus was a herbivore, living on plants. It would have had to eat a huge amount to keep its massive body going, and probably spent most of its waking moments eating. Luckily, the area where it lived was full of lush vegetation. This is the area we now call Patagonia. It would have eaten mostly conifers, seeds, fruit and flowering plants.

The biggest animal ever to live is a modern day giant, the Blue Whale. Argentinosaurus *was* the biggest animal that ever lived on land, though. Its relative, Seismosaurus was actually longer, but less tall, wide and heavy.

Argentinosaurus reigns supreme – at least until the next 'big' discovery!

MEGA FACTS

- A single vertebra (backbone) from Argentinosaurus is taller than a child and measures 1.5m (5 ft) across!

- Argentinosarus was preyed on by the massive meat eater Giganotosaurus and perhaps an even larger recently-discovered meat eater – *Mapusaurus Roseae*, that hunted in packs!

- Thanks to its long neck, Argentinosaurus would have no trouble looking in at a third or fourth storey window.

- In its 'teenage' years when it was growing fastest, Argentinosaurus could gain about 45 kg (100 lb) a day!

- Argentinosaurus was as long as four buses!

DIPLODOCUS

Gigantic long-necked herbivore

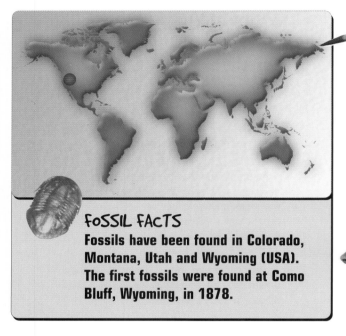

FOSSIL FACTS
Fossils have been found in Colorado, Montana, Utah and Wyoming (USA). The first fossils were found at Como Bluff, Wyoming, in 1878.

Diplodocus means 'double beamed lizard'. It was named in 1878, by Othniel Charles Marsh. The name comes from an unusual feature of the bones in the middle of its tail, where twin extensions of protruding bone run backward and forward. They would have protected blood vessels in the tail if it dragged on the floor, or if the dinosaur pressed its tail against the floor to help balance while rearing on its back legs.

Diplodocus skeleton

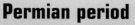

Permian period	Triassic period	Jurassic period	Cretaceous period
(290-248 million years ago)	(248-176 million years ago)	(176-130 million years ago)	(130-66 million years ago)

Appearance

Diplodocus was one of the longest land animals that ever lived. At 27 m (89 ft) long it was a true giant. It stood around 6 m (20 ft) high at the hip and weighed 10,000–11,000 kg (10–11 tons). Diplodocus had hollow bones and so it weighed only an eighth of the similar-sized Brachiosaurus.

Much of its length was accounted for by its long neck and even longer whip-like tail. Its head was tiny, with an elongated snout and nostril on the top of the skull.

In 1990, a new Diplodocus skeleton was found with skin impressions. This suggests diplodocus had row of spines down its back.

MEGA FACTS

- The life-sized replica of diplodocus, named 'Dippy', stands outside the Carnegie Museum of Natural History in Pittsburgh (USA).

- Some scientists believe Diplodocus could swing its long tail as a weapon. If so, the speed at the very tip of the tail would have broken the sound barrier!

Brain

Diplodocus had a brain the size of a fist. It was once thought that Diplodocus had two brains, one in the skull and one close to the base of the spine. Actually, this second 'brain' was simply a concentration of nerves that helped to control the back legs and tail.

Scientists believe Diplodocus could not lift its head very far from the ground. The longer neck may have allowed Diplodocus to push its neck and head a good distance into overgrown forest areas to find food. It could also swing the neck from side to side, allowing it to graze on a wide area without actually moving. Scientists think that Diplodocus would have spent almost every waking moment eating, just to keep its massive body going.

It was a quadruped. Each pillar-like leg had five toes, and one toe on each foot had a thumb claw, which might have been used for self-defence.

Diet

Diplodocus was a herbivore. Its main food would have been conifer leaves and ferns. Its simple, peg-like teeth could strip soft foliage like ferns but couldn't chew them up. Diplodocus swallowed small stones (called gastroliths) to help grind up its food in its stomach.

Dinosaur Data

PRONUNCIATION:	DIP-**LOD**-OH-KUS
SUBORDER:	SAUROPODOMORPHA
FAMILY:	DILODOCIDAE
DESCRIPTION:	LONG-NECKED HERBIVORE
FEATURES:	LONG NECK, WHIPLASH TAIL, HOLLOW BONES, TINY HEAD
DIET:	FERNS AND CONIFERS

APATOSAURUS

Formerly known as Brontosaurus

PLANT EATERS

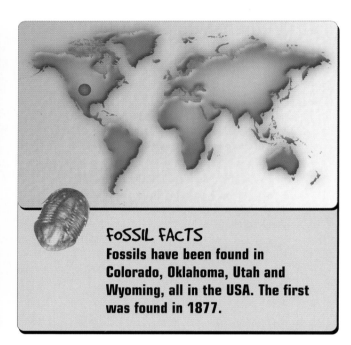

FOSSIL FACTS
Fossils have been found in Colorado, Oklahoma, Utah and Wyoming, all in the USA. The first was found in 1877.

Apatosaurus means 'deceptive lizard'. In 1877, American palaeontologist Othniel C. Marsh described and named a dinosaur called Apatosaurus. In 1879, he described and named another set of dinosaur remains, and – believing them to be from a different creature – christened them Brontosaurus.

Appearance

In 1903, it was discovered that Brontosaurus was in fact simply a fully-grown Apatosaurus! However, the name Brontosaurus was not officially removed from lists until 1974, and it is still popular with many people.

Apatosaurus was some 21–27 m (69–90 ft) long, 3–4.6 m (10–15 ft) tall at the hip and weighed 27,000 kg (27 tons). Its head was tiny at only 60 cm (2 ft) in length. Its long neck had 15 vertebrae, and a long, whip-like tail which accounted for 15 m (50 ft) of its whole length. In the front part of its jaw were peg-like teeth, ideal for stripping leaves and browsing on vegetation. Apatosaurus would have had to eat almost constantly when awake – fortunately, nostrils placed on the top of the skull meant it could eat and breathe at the same time.

Apatosaurus swallowed its food without chewing it, and to help with its digestion, it swallowed stones which stayed in its gizzard. Stones swallowed for this purpose are called gastroliths.

A study in 1999 used computer modelling to test the mobility of the neck of Apatosaurus. The results showed that they could not have lifted their heads any higher than 3–4m (10–13 ft) (just a little higher than their backs), and must most of the time have held their heads downwards or straight out. (They could move their heads freely from side to side, though.)

Dinosaur Data

PRONUNCIATION:	A-**PAT**-OH-**SAWR**-US
SUBORDER:	SAUROPODA
FAMILY:	DIPLODOCIDAE
DESCRIPTION:	LARGE, SLOW-MOVING HERBIVORE
FEATURES:	THICK LEGS, TINY HEAD, LONG NECK, LONG THIN TAIL
DIET:	HERBIVORE: LEAVES, PLANTS, MOSSES

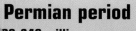

Permian period	Triassic period	Jurassic period	Cretaceous period
90-248 million years ago)	(248-176 million years ago)	(176-130 million years ago)	(130-66 million years ago)

The biggest predator around at the time, Allosaurus, was only 4.6 m (15 ft) tall – an Apatosaurus whose head was raised even by this limited amount would place its head 5.4 m (18 ft) off the ground, making it almost impossible for the carnivore to attack its head and neck.

Like other sauropods, Apatosaurus young hatched from huge eggs. It is assumed that Apatosaurus laid their eggs as they walked, and did not take care of their eggs.

Apatosaurus

MEGA FACTS

- Brain the size of a large apple.

- In the 1933 film *King Kong*, an Apatosaurus was depicted as a bloodthirsty carnivore – quite unlike the gentle plant-eating giant it really was.

- Apatosaurus had thick skin to protect it. Just as well – one of its vertebrae was found with Allosaurus tooth marks in it!

- Fossilised Apatosaurus footprints have been found that measured more than a metre across!

Apatosaurus skeleton

SEISMOSAURUS

Giant whip-tailed herbivore

Seismosaurus means 'earthquake lizard' or 'earth shaker lizard', named because a creature of its fantastic size must have surely shaken the Earth as it walked. It was discovered in 1979, and described and named by David D. Gillette in 1991. Because of its huge size, and the rocks in which it was found, it took 13 years to excavate.

Seismosaurus is currently thought to be the longest animal that ever lived. Its length was estimated originally at around 52 m (170 ft) – in 2004, this was revised to 33.5 m (110 ft). This still leaves Seismosaurus at the top of the 'longest dinosaur' list, and just ahead of the previous longest-ever animal, the blue whale (30.5 m or 100 ft). It probably weighed nearly 45,000 kg (45 tons).

All our information about Seismosaurus comes from the fossilised bones from the hip and part of the back, which were found in 1979. Found mingled with the fossilised bones were the fossilised remains of more than 200 'gastroliths' – small stones that Seismosaurus swallowed to help it digest its food. It is possible that the death of this specimen was caused when it swallowed a particularly large stone, which stuck in its throat and blocked its airway.

Seismosaurus hallorum

Seismosaurus

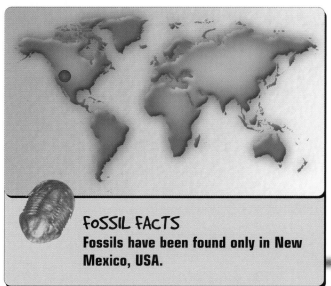

FOSSIL FACTS
Fossils have been found only in New Mexico, USA.

Appearance

Seismosaurus would have looked very like a large Diplodocus, and may not have been much taller, as it had short legs compared to its body length. It had four pillar-like legs with five-toed feet like an elephant, a long neck, and a long, thin tail to counterbalance neck and head. Its head was tiny compared to its length, and housed a very small brain.

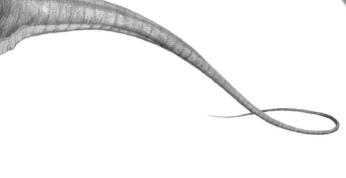

MEGA FACTS

- Probably hatched from eggs like other sauropods.

- Seismosaurus may have lived to be 100 years old.

- Seismosaurus remains are so similar to those of Diplodocus, some scientists think Seismosaurus may not be a separate type of dinosaur at all, but a big new version of Diplodocus.

It had peg-like teeth in the front part of its mouth, ideally suited for stripping the leaves from trees and grazing on plants. It had nostrils on the top of its skull, which allowed it to eat and breathe at the same time. It may have used the whip-like tail for protection.

Seismosaurus' long neck would have usually been held parallel to the ground. It might have allowed the creature to poke its head into dense forest areas to reach leaves otherwise inaccessible to the bulky dinosaurs, or maybe to eat soft pterodophytes that grew in wet areas too swampy to enter safely. Its main diet item was probably conifers, huge forests of which flourished in its time.

Dinosaur Data

PRONUNCIATION:	SIZE-MOH-**SAWR**-US
SUBORDER:	SAUROPODOMORPHA
FAMILY:	DIPLODOCIDAE
DESCRIPTION:	INCREDIBLY LONG HERBIVORE
FEATURES:	LONG NECK, TINY HEAD, WHIP-LIKE TAIL
DIET:	LEAVES, FERNS, MOSSES

HADROSAURUS

Duck-billed browsing herbivore

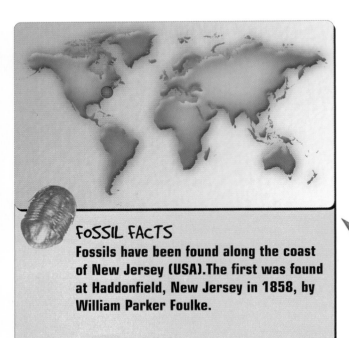

FOSSIL FACTS
Fossils have been found along the coast of New Jersey (USA).The first was found at Haddonfield, New Jersey in 1858, by William Parker Foulke.

Appearance and diet

Hadrosaurus was a herbivore that browsed along the shrub lands and marshes of the Atlantic coast of America 84–71 million years ago. It had a bulky body, stiff tail, and hoof-like nails on its four feet. It was a good swimmer, and may have ventured substantial distances from shore; it could also have spent time in the warm waters. It grew to between 7–10 m (23–30 ft) in length, and 3–4 m (10–13 ft) high – taller than a house if it stood on its back legs! It weighed 1,900 kg (4,000 lb).

Hadrosaurus means 'heavy lizard'. It was studied and named by palaeontologist Joseph Leidy in 1858.

When Hadrosaurus was discovered, it was the most complete dinosaur skeleton that had been found. During the 1800s, various specimens of fossilised bones unlike those of any living animal, and much, much bigger, had been found in Europe and North America.

In 1841, Dr Richard Owen, a British authority on anatomy, suggested these bones belonged to a group of large reptiles, all of which had completely died out long ago. It was he who first coined the name 'dinosaurs', meaning 'terrible lizards'. Until Hadrosaurus came along, though, no one was able to say what one of these 'dinosaurs' would have looked like.

The remains dug up in 1858 included, for the first time, enough of a dinosaur's skeleton to document its anatomy. It was also the first dinosaur fossil ever mounted and put on display in a museum. The study of dinosaurs became a well-respected science.

Hadrosaurus

*Statue of
Hadrosaurus*

MEGA FACTS

- Even though Hadrosuarus had a whole dinosaur family named after it, no Hadrosaurus skull has ever been discovered. The shape of its head is deduced from the skulls of other duck-billed dinosaurs.

- In October 2003, a life-size statue of Hadrosaurus, cast in bronze, was unveiled in Haddonfield, close to the place the first Hadrosaurus was found.

- State Official – in 1991, Hadrosaurus became the official 'state dinosaur' of New Jersey.

Its back legs were longer than its front legs, and this at first led scientists to believe it spent most of its time on its hind legs, in a kind of 'kangaroo-like' stance. We now know that it spent most of its time on all fours. The most recent evidence suggests that Hadrosaurus held its whole rear body aloft, to balance it as it leaned its upper body forward in movements similar to those of modern birds. The front limbs would have been used for foraging.

Dinosaur Data

PRONUNCIATION:	**HAD**-ROW-**SAWR**-US
SUBORDER:	ORNITOPODA
FAMILY:	HADROSAURIDAE
DESCRIPTION:	MASSIVE DUCK-BILLED HERBIVORE
FEATURES:	BULKY BODY, TOOTHLESS BEAK
DIET:	LEAVES, TWIGS

MELANOROSAURUS

Giant herbivorous dinosaur

FOSSIL FACTS
Fossils were found in South Africa in 1924 by Sydney H. Haugh.

Melanorosaurus means 'Black Mountain lizard' and comes from the Greek words *melanos* (black), *oros* (mountain) and *sauros* (lizard). It was named by the British palaeontologist Sydney H. Haugh in 1924 after the Thaba Nyama or Black Mountain in South Africa where the fossil was found.

Melanorosaurus

Appearance

Melanorosaurus lived in the early Triassic period. At 12 m (39 ft) long, 4.3 m (14 ft) tall and probably weighing around 2250 kg (5,000 lb), it was the largest land animal of its time.

Like all sauropods, Melanorosaurus was herbivorous and had a bulky body, long neck and tail, a relatively small skull and brain and erect limbs reminiscent of the limbs of elephants. For some time it was believed that Melanorosaurus was a quadruped, as were many of the giant sauropods.

However, recently scientists have speculated that the sturdy hind limbs with their strong, dense bones could have enabled the creature to walk on its two hind legs, a theory that is given extra weight by the fact that the fore limbs were rather shorter than the hind limbs.

This ability to walk on two legs would make it a facultative biped, a creature that *could* walk on two legs but didn't have to – it may well have taken advantage of this ability to rear up on its hind legs in its quest for tasty leaves!

MEGA FACTS

- Biggest dinosaur of the Triassic era! At 12 m (39 ft) long, Melanorosaurus was the largest dinosaur of its day – only in the Cretaceous period and later have larger dinosaurs been found.

- So far no Melanorosaurus skull has been discovered. However it is believed that its skull would have been very similar in shape to those of the other giant sauropods, many of whose skulls have been found.

- Whilst its limbs had dense bones, its spinal bones and vertebrae had hollows to reduce their weight.

Diet

Melanorosaurus' diet would have consisted of branches, leaves and twigs, with its height and long neck allowing it to easily reach the tops of trees. Taking large mouthfuls of food at a time, it would use its serrated leaf-shaped teeth to snap off branches and then chew the vegetation quite effectively before swallowing. Its long neck meant it could browse over a sizeable area by just moving its head and neck, this allowed it to reduce the amount of energy it would have to use up in moving – important when considering how much energy from plants it would take to maintain such a large body.

Dinosaur Data

PRONUNCIATION:	MEL-UH-**NOR**-UH-**SAWR**-US
SUBORDER:	SAUROPODOMORPHA
FAMILY:	MELANOROSAURIDAE
DESCRIPTION:	GIANT LONG-NECKED **HERBIVORE**
FEATURES:	LONG NECK AND TAIL, BULKY BODY, LEAF-SHAPED SERRATED TEETH
DIET:	BRANCHES, LEAVES AND TWIGS

SALTASAURUS

Armour-plated herbivore

FOSSIL FACTS
Fossils have been found in Argentina and Uruguay (South America). The first specimen was found in the north-western Argentinian province of Salta, in 1970.

Dinosaur Data

PRONUNCIATION:	SALT-AH-**SAWR**-US
SUBORDER:	SAUROPODOMORPHA
FAMILY:	TITANOSAURIDAE
DESCRIPTION:	ARMOURED SAUROPOD
FEATURES:	BONY ARMOUR PLATES ON BACK AND SIDES
DIET:	LOW-GROWING FERNS, LEAVES

Permian period	Triassic period	Jurassic period	Cretaceous period
290-248 million years ago)	(248-176 million years ago)	(176-130 million years ago)	(130-66 million years ago)

Saltasaurus means 'lizard from Salta'. It is named after the Argentinian province of Salta where it was found by José Bonaparte and Jaime Powell in 1980.

Appearance

Saltsaurus was a sauropod, 12 m (40 ft) long and weighed 7,000 kg (7 tons). It had a bulky body, four stout legs ending in five-toed feet, a long neck ending in a tiny head, and a stout tail that tapered to whiplash thinness.

Its neck was shorter than that of most sauropods, but would still have helped it to feed on vegetation out of the reach of shorter herbivores. It had blunt teeth, in the back part of its mouth only. Some scientists believe it could rear up on its hind legs for short periods of time, perhaps using its tail for extra support and balance.

Saltasaurus lived about 70–65 million years ago. In most parts of the world at this time, sauropod dinosaurs were giving way to the more successful duck-billed dinosaurs.

South America, though, was an island continent and life evolved there somewhat differently. The duckbills never made much of an impression there, and sauropods continued to evolve there long after they had largely died out elsewhere.

MEGA FACTS

- A large nesting ground discovered in 1997 may have belonged to Saltasaurus. Remains showed that several hundred holes and been dug and eggs about 11–12 cm (4–5 in.) in diameter laid in them. The nests were then buried under dirt and vegetation to conceal them from predators.

- Communal nest building shows that Saltasaurus probably lived and travelled in herds.

- Saltasaurus eggs had a shell 6 mm (¼ in.) thick.

Armour plating

This may explain the most distinctive feature of Saltasaurus – unlike any previously-found sauropods, it had armour plating! Its back and sides were covered in circular and oval bony plates, up to 12 cm (5 in.) in diameter. It is thought horns or spikes may have stuck out from these plates, but firm evidence for this is yet to be found.

The discovery of Saltasaurus completely changed the way scientists thought about the sauropods. It had been assumed until then that the sauropods' size alone was enough to protect them from predators – so when Titanosaurus remains were found with armour plates, it had been reclassified as an ankylosaur. Saltasaurus showed that a dinosaur could have armour *and* still be a sauropod, and Titanosaurus was returned to the sauropod fold.

TITANOSAURUS

Giant armoured herbivore

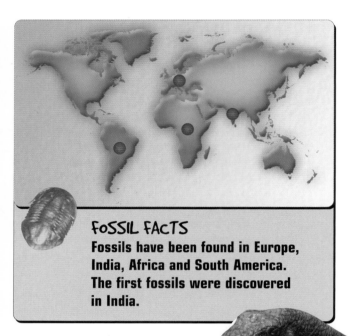

FOSSIL FACTS
Fossils have been found in Europe, India, Africa and South America. The first fossils were discovered in India.

Titanosaurus means 'titanic lizard'. The dinosaur was named by Richard Lydekker in 1877 – almost 20 years after its remains were first discovered.

Titanosaurus was a sauropod dionosaur, like Argentinosaurus and Brachiosaurus.

Appearance

Titanosaurus had a bulky body, a long 'whiplash' tail and a tiny head on the end of its long neck. The head was incredibly small compared to the rest of its body, but was quite wide. It had large nostrils, and its nasal bones formed a sort of raised crest on its skull. It had very small teeth.

It grew to around 12–18 m (39–59 ft) in length and about 3–5 m (10–16 ft) tall at the hips. It would have weighed about 14,700 kg (15 tons).

This dinosaur walked on all fours. Its front legs were stout and stocky. Its back legs were longer than the front ones, and Titanosaurus would have been able to rear up onto these strong back legs to reach higher up trees for food. It had a very flexible spine, making rearing up easy.

Dinosaur Data

PRONUNCIATION:	TIE-**TAN**-OH-**SAWR**-US
SUBORDER:	SAUROPODA
FAMILY:	TITANOSAURIDAE
DESCRIPTION:	GIANT ARMOURED HERBIVORE
FEATURES:	LONG NECK, FLEXIBLE BACK, ARMOURED SKIN
DIET:	CONIFERS, PALMS, GRASSES

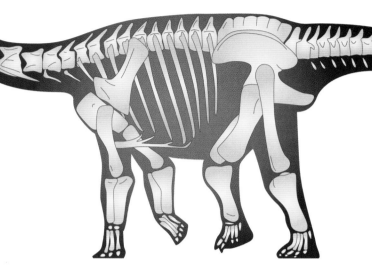

Titanosaurus had a very wide chest, which placed its legs and feet widely apart. Scientists have discovered fossilised footprints (we call these 'fossilised trackways') showing that Titanosaurus tracks are much wider than those of other sauropod dinosaurs.

Fosssilised impressions of Titanosaurus' skin have survived, so we know that it had armour to protect it. Its skin was covered with a pattern of small 'bead-like' scales surrounding larger scales.

Diet

The fossilised remains of Titanosaur dung show that Titanosaurus had quite a broad diet. It ate pretty much any plant material – remains from conifer twigs and leaves, palms and grasses were all found. Titanosaurus lived in herds, browsing from place to place to find fresh vegetation to eat.

Reproduction

Titanosaurus laid eggs, and the whole herd probably shared one large nesting ground, where they dug nests and then buried their eggs under dirt and vegetation. Their eggs would have measured only 11–12 cm (4–5 in.) across.

Latest discoveries

In May 2006, Italian scientists announced the discovery of four well-preserved Titanosaur skeletons in South America. There are skeletons of young Titanosaurs as well as adults.

MEGA FACTS

- Although Titanosaurus eggs were only about 12 cm (5 in.) across, the babies that hatched would grow to be longer than a bus!

- Living in herds would have given Titanosaurus protection against large predators.

NODOSAURUS

Tank-like armoured herbivore

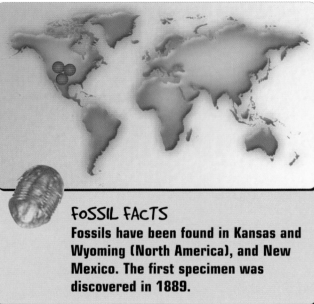

FOSSIL FACTS
Fossils have been found in Kansas and Wyoming (North America), and New Mexico. The first specimen was discovered in 1889.

Appearance

Nodosaurus was 4–6 m (13–20 ft) long and grew up to 3 m (10 ft) high. It moved on four stocky legs, and had five-toed feet. Its front legs were much shorter than its back legs, making its body strongly arched. Its neck was short and its head small.

No Nodosaurus skull has been discovered so its shape has to be deduced from skulls of other nodosaurids. It would probably have had a narrow head, a pointed snout, and powerful jaws with small leaf-shaped teeth back in its cheeks. It may have fed on soft plants. Like other herbivores, it may have swallowed small stones (called gastroliths) to aid with grinding up food in its large gut.

Nodosaurus means 'knobbed lizard' or 'node lizard'. It was named by Othniel Charles Marsh in 1889, and takes its name from the bony armour plates and knobs which covered most of its skin. Bony armour plates like those possessed by nodosaurus are called scutes. It gave its name to the group of ankylosaurs called nodosaurids.

Nodosaurids differ from the other types of ankylosaur in lacking a club at the end of their tail. Nodosaurids were distinguished by the bands of spikes that ran along the sides of their body, pear-shaped heads, and relatively narrow toothless beaks. A bony plate separated their nasal passage from their mouth, so that they could chew food and breathe at the same time.

They had a single large armour plate over the snout, and a solid shield of partially-fused armoured plates protecting the pelvic area. For extra protection, they had bony spikes that stuck out from their flanks.

Nodosaurus attacked by lone raptor

Permian period (290-248 million years ago)	Triassic period (248-176 million years ago)	Jurassic period (176-130 million years ago)	Cretaceous period (130-66 million years ago)

Defence

It had armour plating on its back and sides. It had large armoured plates topped with bony nodes on the skin between its ribs, and – unlike other nodosaurids – had dorsal armour, consisting of a pair of midline rectangular scutes with domed centres alternating with bands of smaller, flat and square-shaped scutes. It may have had shoulder or side spikes – remains found so far are not enough to tell us for certain.

Nodosaurus had little means of attacking an enemy. If attacked, it probably relied on crouching low to the ground to protect its soft underside.

MEGA FACTS

- Nodosorous had a small head and minuscule brain compared to the size of its body, indicating very low intelligence.

- In 2003, the fossilised skeleton of an armoured dinosaur that may be a Nodosaurus was found in Kent, England. Except for the missing skull, it is remarkably complete. Only further study will tell us for certain if this is the first Nodosaurus found outside America.

Dinosaur Data

PRONUNCIATION:	NOH-DOH-**SAWR**-US
SUBORDER:	THYREOPHORA
FAMILY:	NODOSAURIDAE
DESCRIPTION:	ARMOURED HERBIVORE

A top view of Nodosaurus's formidable spikes

27

MINMI

Small and unusual armoured herbivore

This dinosaur was named and described by Ralph Molnar in 1980. It was named after the place where the first pieces of its fossil remains had been found, Minmi Crossing.

Minmi was the first armoured dinosaur found south of the equator. It is also the most complete dinosaur skeleton ever found in Australia.

Appearance

Minmi seems to have been a very primitive ankylosaur and scientists have found it hard to classify. It has features in common with both ankylosaurs and nodosaurs, but is not identical to either. Its snout arched higher than the rest of its skull, which is common in nodosaurs. It had armoured plates like an ankylosaur's – but its legs were longer, and it had no 'club' at the end of its tail.

It would have been about the size of a year-old calf, growing to only 2–3 m (6–10 ft) long and about 1 m (3 ft) high, and weighing around 1,700 kg (3,740 lb). Its back legs were longer than its front ones, and it went on all fours. Minmi would have lived on the low-growing plants of the floodplains and woodlands where it roamed.

As well as having longer legs than ankylosaurus, Minmi had extra bony plates added to its backbone. These strengthened its back, helping support the weight of its armour. Extra muscles attached to these extra plates could have allowed Minmi to run at reasonable speed.

Defence

Minmi had skin armoured with large bony plates (called scutes) and smaller pea-sized bones (called ossicles) embedded all over it. Even Minmi's underbelly was protected by small bony plates, which makes it unique among the whole thyreophoran suborder of dinosaurs.

Apart from this armour, Minmi had no real way to defend itself – it lacked the tail 'club' possessed by most ankylosaurs. Running away was probably its best defence!

Minmi was the only ankylosaur to have paravertebrae. Some scientists have suggested that these are actually tendons which have ossified (changed into bone) rather than true bones.

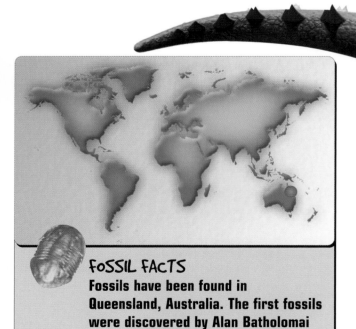

FOSSIL FACTS
Fossils have been found in Queensland, Australia. The first fossils were discovered by Alan Batholomai near Roma, Queensland in 1964.

PLANT EATERS

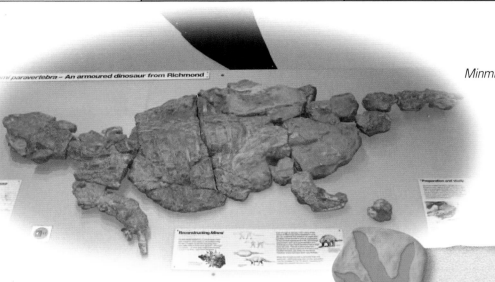

mi paravertebra – An armoured dinosaur from Richmond

Minmi skeleton

Minmi has much in common with both ankylosaurs and nodosaurs, but it may turn out to be a wholly new type of armoured dinosaur!

MEGA FACTS

- In 1990 an almost-complete Minmi skeleton was found in Queensland. It was so well preserved that wrinkles in its skin could be made out from the pattern of the ossicles.

- Minmi has the shortest name ever given to a dinosaur.

- Recent studies have been able to analyse the contents of a Minmi stomach. It was able to chew its food into smaller pieces before swallowing them.

Dinosaur Data

PRONUNCIATION:	**MIN**-MEE
SUBORDER:	THYREOPHORA
DESCRIPTION:	SMALL ARMOURED HERBIVORE
FEATURES:	ARMOURED PLATES ON BELLY
DIET:	LOW-GROWING SOFT PANTS MATERIALS, LEAVES, FRUIT, STEMS

CAMARASAURUS

Giant herbivore

FOSSIL FACTS
Camarasaurus fossils have been found in North America.
Ultrasaurus fossils have been found in the USA and Asia.

Dinosaur Data

PRONUNCIATION:	KUH-**MARE**-UH-**SAWR**-US
SUBORDER:	SAUROPODOMORPHA
FAMILY:	CAMARASAURIDAE
DESCRIPTION:	A GIANT HERBIVORE
FEATURES:	SPOON-SHAPED TEETH
DIET:	PLANTS

Camarasaurus lived during the
late Jurassic Period, about
155 to 145 million
years ago.

Camarasaurus looked very much like
Diplodocus with its long neck and tail. It was
a giant herbivore, but it wasn't as big as
other sauropods. It still weighed up to
20,000 kg (20 tons)!

Its head was small and long, and it had a blunt snout. It had
spoon-shaped teeth, which were ideal for munching on
leaves and branches.

Camarasaurus fossils have been found in groups with both
adult and young together. They probably traveled together in
herds like elephants.